REFINER'S FIRE

Living in a World of Compromise

by
Rod Parsley

Harrison House
Tulsa, Oklahoma

Refiner's Fire — Living in a World of Compromise
ISBN 0-89274-903-2
Copyright © 1992 by Rod Parsley
World Harvest Church
P. O. Box 32932
Columbus, Ohio 43232

Published by Harrison House, Inc.
P. O. Box 35035
Tulsa, Oklahoma 74153

Contents

Introduction

Abstain from all appearance of evil.

And the very God of peace sanctify you wholly; and I pray God your whole spirit and soul and body be preserved blameless unto the coming of our Lord Jesus Christ.

1 Thessalonians 5:22, 23

God created man in perfect innocence. The devil came along and introduced man to sin. Sin separated man from God. But God had a plan to destroy sin and offer man a way back from sin and to Himself. Jesus came — God in the flesh — to destroy sin in the flesh and offer man the way back into fellowship with a holy God.

God is calling His people — His Church — to come out of the world and be separate. He calls us to sanctify ourselves and be holy as He is holy.

When we are born again, we are like raw material — like crude oil that just came from the ground. Crude oil cannot go right out of the ground into our automobile engines. Crude oil has to be refined and purified into gasoline.

God is refining and purifying His Church in this hour. He is washing us in the water of the Word and ironing us with the pressure and fire of the Holy Spirit. He is taking out the spots and wrinkles and making a glorious Church that is overcoming in every area, trampling the gates of hell under its feet and exalting the name of Jesus in the earth. But in order for Him to do that, we must be *sanctified*.

What is this thing we call sanctification? It is an act of divine grace, whereby we are made holy. When we are born

5

again, we get a new spirit and a new life. But we are not immune to the tempter. We can still sin. Sanctification is when we allow God to separate us from the world and its ways and walk a life set apart and holy unto Him.

Sanctification is *not* outward appearances such as hair styles, dress codes and make-up. Sanctification is a matter of the heart, where we lay down our lives, take up our cross and follow Jesus, whatever the cost. It is a hatred for sin that refuses to compromise with the world or the devil in any way.

Sanctification is an understanding that when we *do* sin, we have an advocate with the Father, Jesus Christ. But for Jesus to be our advocate, we have to learn how to operate in our relationship with Him. It is more than an apology — it hinges on *repentance*. We need to see the New Testament doctrine of repentance restored to the Church by a generation of preachers and saints who will repair the breach and restore paths of righteousness to dwell in.

The Church must arise and address the problem of sin in her midst. If a man slaps his wife before he is born again, we call it sin and tell him he needs to repent and be saved. If a man who has come to the altar and been born again slaps his wife, we call it his "problem" and send him to counseling.

What the American Church needs is less counseling and more churches filled with the *fire* of God. We need people living holy lives before God so that the presence of God can flood into the midst of them and bring the convicting power of the Holy Spirit.

We need conviction, not condemnation! When sanctification was preached in the past, it was often a message of condemnation. But God does not condemn His people. He sends the Holy Spirit to *convict* people. The devil is the one who condemns.

Jesus, in His prayer in John 17, said,

I have given them thy word; and the world hath hated them, because they are not of the world, even as I am not of the world.

I pray not that thou shouldest take them out of the world, but that thou shouldest keep them from the evil.

They are not of the world, even as I am not of the world.

Sanctify them through thy truth: thy word is truth.

As thou hast sent me into the world, even so have I also sent them into the world.

And for their sakes I sanctify myself, that they also might be sanctified through the truth.

Neither pray I for these alone, but for them also which shall believe on me through their word;

That they may all be one; as thou, Father, art in me, and I in thee, that they also may be one in us: that the world may believe that thou hast sent me.

John 17:14-21

Jesus prayed for His disciples and all those who would believe on Him through the preaching of the disciples that we all be one, and that we be set apart, sanctified, holy.

My prayer is that this book will sound as a trumpet call in the spirit realm to awaken the Church to return to true holiness — holiness that comes by allowing the Spirit of God and the Word of God to penetrate the thoughts and intents of our hearts and remove all that is offensive to Him.

GOD IS PREPARING
A HOUSE FOR
HIS GLORY

1

God Is Preparing a House for His Glory

The voice of him that crieth in the wilderness, Prepare ye the way of the Lord, make straight in the desert a highway for our God.

Every valley shall be exalted, and every mountain and hill shall be made low: and the crooked shall be made straight, and the rough places plain:

And the glory of the Lord shall be revealed, and all flesh shall see it together: for the mouth of the Lord hath spoken it.

Isaiah 40:3-5

For the earth shall be filled with the knowledge of the glory of the Lord, as the waters cover the sea.

Habakkuk 2:14

The glory of this latter house shall be greater than of the former, saith the Lord of hosts: and in this place will I give peace, saith the Lord of hosts.

Haggai 2:9

God is preparing His Church for His glory! The prophets prophesied it over and over. The desire of the Father's heart is for His glory to cover the earth. But first He must begin with His Church.

He is preparing us for glory. Paul wrote in 2 Corinthians 4:17, **For our light affliction, which is but for a moment, worketh for us a far more exceeding and eternal weight of glory.**

9

The shaking in the Church and the earth today is preparing us to carry God's glory.

> **For other foundation can no man lay than that is laid, which is Jesus Christ.**
>
> **Now if any man build upon this foundation gold, silver, precious stones, wood, hay, stubble;**
>
> **Every man's work shall be made manifest; for the day shall declare it, because it shall be revealed by fire; and the fire shall try every man's work of what sort it is.**
>
> **1 Corinthians 3:11-13**
>
> **But we have this treasure in earthen vessels, that the excellency of the power may be of God, and not of us.**
>
> **We are troubled on every side, yet not distressed; we are perplexed, but not in despair;**
>
> **Persecuted, but not forsaken; cast down, but not destroyed;**
>
> **Always bearing about in the body the dying of the Lord Jesus, that the life also of Jesus might be made manifest in our mortal flesh.**
>
> **2 Corinthians 4:7-10**

The treasure that we have is the very presence of God in manifestation in our mortal bodies. We pray and cry out to God that we want to manifest His glory. If we truly desire to see His glory, we must understand this one thing — *the glory that is seen and perceived becomes the glory revealed.* We will never reveal any more of the glory of God than we have seen. Paul said in 2 Corinthians 3:18: **But we all, with open face beholding as in a glass the glory of the Lord, are changed into the same image from glory to glory, even as by the Spirit of the Lord.**

Hebrews 12:14 tells us that without holiness, no man will see the Lord. Holiness — sanctification — is *required* for the manifestation of the glory of God in the Church. The glory of God will not come where there is sin. It would consume the sin and the sinner! We *must* get the sin out of the camp — out of our individual lives and out of the Church — if we ever expect the glory of the Lord to fill His temple.

The Church today has a lot of *doing* and very little *seeing*. We go on in our own endeavors. We've defined what we think ministry ought to be. We've defined how we think the Church ought to be. We've told God what He ought to do in our lives. We've lined it all out for Him and taken His Word and told Him what He should do in our lives.

But God is building *Himself* a house, a habitation, a place to dwell. He did it under the Old Covenant — He built a tabernacle, and the Holy of Holies, and came down to dwell among His people.

Now He wants to build a house out of *people*. Peter says we are **...lively stones... built up a spiritual house, an holy priesthood, to offer up spiritual sacrifices, acceptable to God by Christ Jesus** (1 Pet. 2:5).

God wants to build a tabernacle of lively, *living* stones in which He can dwell. But all too often, we don't want to *let* Him build His house. We want Him to dwell with us all right, but *we* want to design and build the house and then invite God to move in. But God says *no!* He will build His own house. *He* is the potter — *we* are the clay. *He* does the molding, and we *allow* Him, of our own *free will* and *complete trust*, to mold us however He desires.

God, in His Church corporately and in us individually, is building Himself a dwelling place. Why? So He can manifest His glory in us. Paul told the Colossian church that the mystery hidden for ages and now revealed to the saints is **Christ in you, the hope of glory** (Col. 1:27).

Ephesians 2:20-22, speaking of the Church, says:

> **And are built upon the foundation of the apostles and prophets, Jesus Christ himself being the chief corner stone;**

In whom all the building fitly framed together groweth unto an holy temple in the Lord:

In whom ye also are builded together for an habitation of God through the Spirit.

But we will only manifest the glory that we have beheld. *Glory beheld becomes glory revealed.* Jesus did not say, "Whatever I want to do, I go and do it and then ask the Father to bless it." He said, "I wait. I watch the Father. Whatever I see the Father do, that's what I do."

There are things in our lives God wants to take out and other things He wants to put in. The only way He can do what He wants in our lives is for us to *allow* Him to. We must place our lives in the hands of the Master Builder so He can build a place where He can dwell. God dwells in our *hearts*, and many Christians have closed off the door of their hearts to the Lord. We often let hurts of the past, pride or religious tradition keep the door of our heart closed to the Spirit of God.

Many Are Inoculated With Religion

Many Christians get *inoculated* with religion, much the same as people traveling overseas are inoculated to build resistance to diseases. Travelers are given small amounts of the disease — just enough to make them mildly sick — and the body builds a resistance to the real thing.

Religion will do the same thing. It will give us a *taste* of God — just enough to make many people feel good and self-satisfied — and build up a resistance to a really powerful move of the Spirit of God in our lives.

All over the world we have people who have been *inoculated* with religion. What they have is so close to the real thing that many are deceived into believing they *have* the real thing. But God is building *His* house, and He is calling His people to go beyond religion and the traditions of men and allow Him to fashion us as lively stones for His habitation.

The Word Brings Conviction, Not Condemnation

> **To whom shall I speak, and give warning, that they may hear? behold, their ear is uncircumcised, and they cannot hearken: behold, the word of the Lord is unto them a reproach; they have no delight in it.**
>
> **Jeremiah 6:10**

The Word of God was a reproach to the people of Jeremiah's time because it *convicted* them of sin. They said, as does the modern Church, "Don't preach that way. We don't like to hear that kind of preaching. It puts condemnation on us."

If there is one thing the Church today needs to understand, it is the difference between conviction and condemnation. One of the purposes of the Holy Spirit is to *convict* men of sin.

Conviction leads to godly sorrow which leads to repentance. Condemnation drives people *away* from God. Conviction draws people *to* God. Conviction lasts until the person responds to the prompting and prodding of the Holy Spirit that calls them back into line, cleanses the temple, and prepares a habitation for God.

Sin in the Church Must Be Addressed

Some don't want to preach about sin for fear of building sin consciousness in the people. But people — even Christians — do a good job of sinning whether it is preached about or not.

Yes, we need to talk about the goodness, grace and mercy of God. We need to emphasize the positive and build faith in Christians. But if we never preach about sin, Christian people will continue to get ensnared in it, and we will fail to recognize what Jesus is doing in His Church. We will not see and understand when He is trying to purify and cleanse our hearts, motives and methods.

Proverbs 4:23 tells us to **Keep thy heart with all diligence; for out of it are the issues of life.** God wants us to set armed guards around our heart, that no intruder may enter to spoil the dwelling place of God. He wants us to be built up as a holy habitation for His glory. God wants to come and live on the inside of us.

Jesus does not come to cleanse and purify His Church because He is a mean tyrant. He is doing it to build a habitation in which a holy God can dwell forever. He wants us to behold His glory, be filled with His glory and manifest His glory to a hurting, dying, lost world.

Manifested Glory Means Manifested Miracles

We pray for revival, and revival will come. We will see revival such as the world has never seen, where hospitals are emptied out, and sinners run to the altar by the thousands. But it will not happen just because we want it to.

Satan will not relinquish his strongholds just because we think it is a good idea. The only thing the devil understands is for someone to come along with a bigger stick than he is carrying. Jesus *has* that bigger stick. He won it at calvary, and He wants to give it to His Church in full measure. But the only way we will have this level of power flow through us as a Church — the level of power and anointing that converts whole cities and empties hospitals — is for us to get the sin and impurity out so His glory can be manifested.

We Are Changed Into His Likeness

If the Church wants the power of God that will shake nations, we must, individually and corporately, climb the mountain of God and remain in His presence until His glory fills us and radiates from our countenance. Moses climbed Mount Sinai and stayed in the presence of God until the glory was so strong on him the people could not bear to look at him without a veil. (2 Cor. 3:7.)

Paul said the ministry of the Holy Spirit to the Church is *more* glorious than what Moses experienced. (2 Cor. 3:8.) When we turn to the Lord Jesus and behold *His* face, we are changed into His image from glory to glory. (2 Cor. 3:18.)

The problem with much of the Church has been a self-centeredness that builds its own kingdom instead of beholding the face of Jesus and being *changed*. That is why many Christians are powerless against the onslaughts of a pagan society.

The reason God convicts us of sin, and wants to purify us, is so He can come down and live in us and manifest His full glory through us. But all too often we have wanted His glory to be revealed without first *beholding* His glory. God cannot reveal and manifest His glory through us until we get rid of all that separates us from His presence. If His glory were fully revealed in our present state, it would consume most of us.

God wants to cleanse His temple today! He wants to cleanse His Church! It is not a bad thing He desires — it is a *good* thing! It is the *goodness* of God that leads men to repentance. (Rom. 2:4.)

God wants to cleanse His temple, and the Church wants it, also. People are crying out to be told the *truth!* The people of God are tired of being spoon fed and soft-soaped with a gospel of humanism. Those who hunger and thirst after righteousness *want* their sins confronted — they *want* to be holy. If we will *let* God cleanse His temple and *let* Him restore His presence to the Church, He will come as a swift witness and build a habitation where His presence and His glory will abide *forever!*

WHY
HOLINESS?

2

Why Holiness?

**Follow peace with all men, and holiness, without
which no man shall see the Lord.**

Hebrews 12:14

This is a strong statement! If the Holy Spirit inspired
the writer of Hebrews to say no man would see the Lord
without holiness, then we must get serious about the
subject. The church has gone from the extreme of legalism
— judgment based on external measures such as hair,
makeup, jewelry, etc. — to the opposite extreme of
permissiveness. It seems as if anything goes! Many think
nothing of sleeping around on Friday night, then going to
church and praising God Sunday morning!

We love to preach against sin in the world. But are we
any better when we have rampant immorality — adultery,
fornication, homosexuality, to name some of the most
obvious — right in the midst of our "born again, Bible
quoting, Spirit-filled" churches?

Where Is the Conviction of Sin?

Where is the conviction of sin? Paul asked the question
in Romans 6:1, **Shall we continue in sin, that grace may
abound? God forbid. How shall we, that are dead to sin,
live any longer therein?**

The reason sin is so rampant in our midst is that we
have preached an easy Gospel. People are told to raise their
hands, fill out a decision card, and make a mental assent
and they will be welcomed into the Church.

17

The Holy Spirit was sent to convict the world of sin. (John 16:8.) The Holy Spirit prompts us, corrects us and brings us back into alignment with the perfect will of God. He does this so we will be able to manifest the glory of God in the midst of a sin-cursed world.

Man *must* be made to feel the weight of his sin. George Whitfield said, ''Here stands God — forgiveness in one hand and the sword in the other — bidding the sinner to repent and live or refuse and perish.''

We can never receive full forgiveness until we first feel the weight of our sin. That is why we have faulty conversions, many falling away and sin rampant in the Church. Too many people were put on the membership rolls without first being convicted of sin and coming to repentance.

The message to the Body of Christ is, *Repent, for the kingdom of Heaven is at hand*! Repentance is not a negative message! Repentance is a positive message! It is the way the bride of Christ will cleanse herself from all unrighteousness and prepare herself for the coming of the Bridegroom.

Whitfield continued to say, ''Have you ever, in all your life, been sorry for your sins — truly, genuinely overwhelmed with godly sorrow? Has the weight of your sin been so heavy that you could not lift your head for the weight thereof? Have you ever cried out, as did Paul, the apostle, 'Who shall deliver me from this body of death, o wretched man that I am?' ''

The Gospel *Confronts* Sin

The Church must return to a Gospel that *confronts* sin, not *compromises* with it! The Church must return to a Gospel such as Peter preached on the Day of Pentecost, when 3,000 souls cried out in anguish, **Men and brethren, what shall we do?** (Acts 2:37).

We have preached and taught about our authority as believers and our rights and privileges in the kingdom of God. These are true and valid principles. God loves His people and wants them healed and blessed. But in our own pride and presumptuousness, many in the Church have taken the truth of the goodness of God and perverted it into a Gospel of selfishness.

Too often we have reduced God to a formula. Say the right thing, confess this verse so many times, demand this promise, and it is yours. Many Christians see God as a great vending machine, believing that if they put in the right coins, the answer will come bouncing out!

God is not a vending machine! We are called to bear His marks, not to be His manipulator! Our prayers too often become order blanks for everything we want. What happened to ''Not my will, but thine?'' What happened to taking up our *cross* and following Him? How about sharing in His sufferings that we may share in His glory?

The Lord addressed this subject through the prophet Isaiah, as recorded in Isaiah 29:13-16:

> Wherefore the Lord said, Forasmuch as this people draw near me with their mouth, and with their lips do honour me, but have removed their heart far from me, and their fear toward me is taught by the precept of men:

> Therefore, behold, I will proceed to do a marvelous work among this people, even a marvelous work and a wonder: for the wisdom of their wise men shall perish, and the understanding of their prudent men shall be hid.

> Woe unto them that seek deep to hide their counsel from the Lord, and their works are in the dark, and they say, Who seeth us? and who knoweth us?

> Surely your turning of things upside down shall be esteemed as the potter's clay: for shall the work say

of him that made it, He made me not? or shall the thing framed say of him that framed it, He had no understanding?

God is crying out to his people today just as He was in the time of Isaiah: *You honor Me with your lips! You have all the right confessions and scriptures! But where is your heart?* We have turned this thing upside down. The clay is trying to tell the potter what it will be. But that is not the purpose of the clay.

The purpose of the clay is to climb up on the potter's wheel and be quiet! The purpose of the clay is to say, "Mold me, make me. Whatever pressure it takes, and however hot and uncomfortable it must get, it's all right, Lord! I just want to come out the vessel *You* want to make. Have *your* way with this lump of clay, Lord."

What Is Prayer in the Spirit?

Yes, we serve a God who answers prayer. But what is our concept of prayer? Is it just a "give me" session? Prayer should be nothing more or less than direct communication with a loving Father. When we talk to our own fathers, is it always to ask for something? If so, our fathers would soon tire of talking to us. Sometimes we ask for things or counsel, and sometimes we receive comfort. And sometimes we simply tell our earthly fathers how much we love and appreciate them.

Should it be any different with our heavenly Father? Prayer is communion with Him. But since He is a Spirit, the communion must be in the spiritual. Now there is nothing mystical or hocus-pocus about prayer in the spirit — *and it is not always praying in tongues, either*! Prayer in the spirit is simply prayer that is free from the bondage of the intellect. It is a direct line to God, not touching the natural realm.

Prayer in the spirit is allowing the Holy Spirit to direct our prayers, whether they are in our native tongue or in "tongues" inspired by the Holy Ghost. Paul said in Romans 8:26 that we don't even know how to pray or what to pray for. We think we know, but we don't know. That's why we have the Holy Spirit to help us pray.

Prayer Is Relationship

The point I am trying to make is that prayer is relationship. We have rightly understood that God is bound by His Word, and in our self-worship, we have often attempted to turn God into a vending machine. Yes, God delights in the prosperity of His people. Yes, God wants His people healed and blessed and free from anxiety and care. But most of all, He wants *relationship* with His children. He wants us to come to Him on the basis of who *He* is, not who *we* are.

There has been so much emphasis in the Body of Christ on who *we* are in Christ, that many have taken it too far and forgotten Who *Christ* is in us — *the hope of glory*. We get so caught up in building our churches and businesses and in meeting our personal needs that we forget to stop and consider what *God* wants and needs.

This is not a democracy! The Church is not a fast food restaurant! We can't have it our way! The kingdom of God is a monarchy where Jesus is the absolute Monarch, ruling by divine authority. The kingdom of God is a theocracy, with *One God* in charge. God has a plan and purpose for this earth, and it is bigger than any one person, group, church or movement. If we want the blessings of God — if we want true relationship with God — then we must spend less time with our want list and more time seeking His will.

Yes, God is bound by His Word. But that is not so we can take His Word and manipulate Him. God is *sovereign*.

Not one jot or tittle of His Word — not one dot of the "i" or cross of the "t" will fall void of power. Every word of God will accomplish what it is sent to do, but His Word will be fulfilled according to *His* wisdom, *not ours.*

Why Prayers Are Not Answered

The reason many of our prayers are not answered is because we ask amiss. (James 4:30.) Simply stated, that means we ask with wrong, evil or selfish motives. In other words, we want *our* will above the will of God.

If we speak to the mountain and it moves, according to Mark 11:22-24, it is because we are in the flow of God's will — *not* because we found that scripture and decided we could move any mountain in our way. If you spoke to the mountain and it did not move, check your heart! Check your motives! Are you building your kingdom, or God's? Did Jesus, the Head of the Church, put you on television, or are you trying to build your own ministry? Did the Holy Spirit lead you into that business, or is greed your motivation?

Paul wrote in Philippians 2:13, **For it is God which worketh in you both to will and to do of his good pleasure.** *That* is the key. It is God, *working in you*, both to will and to do of *His* good pleasure. So when we pray and the mountain moves, it is because our will has been lined up with God's will.

Holiness Reveals the Will of God

What is the will of God for you? If you are living a holy, consecrated life, walking in the presence of God and led by the Spirit of God, then whatever wells up inside of your spirit is the will of God. We have the written Word as a standard and the Holy Spirit within to check us when we are going astray and to guide us into all truth. So it is not a great mystery.

The problem comes when Christians compromise with the world and allow impurity and unrighteousness into their hearts and lives. Sin will always grieve the Holy Spirit and cause Him to withdraw. Without Him, we have lost our guide. We have no compass — no warning of wrong or confirmation of right. The result is sin pervading the Church as much as it is pervading the world.

When the Church stops preaching holiness, the door opens for sin to abound. Why is there greed, backstabbing, selfish ambition and blatant immorality in the pulpit and the pew? It happens when we stop preaching holiness; we fail to set a standard to measure against.

When I say *holiness,* I'm not referring to outward externals of hair, makeup and jewelry. Paul forever destroyed the emphasis on externals in his letter to the Colossians:

> **If then you have died with Christ to material ways of looking at things and have escaped from the world's crude and elemental notions and teachings of externalism, why do you live as if you still belong to the world? Why do you submit to rules and regulations? [such as],**
>
> **Do not handle [this], Do not taste [that], Do not even touch [them],**
>
> **Referring to things all of which perish with being used. To do this is to follow human precepts and doctrines.**
>
> **Such [practices] have indeed the outward appearance [that popularly passes] for wisdom, in promoting self-imposed rigor of devotion and delight in self-humiliation and severity of discipline of the body, but they are of no value in checking the indulgence of the flesh — the lower nature. [Instead, they do not honor God] but serve only to indulge the flesh.**
>
> **Colossians 2:20-23 AMP**

We are separate and different from animals because we have a spirit. What separates us from the world is that we have a recreated, or "born again" human spirit. God wants us to worship Him in our spirits, not our souls. The soul gets involved, but the worship must flow from the spirit.

God cannot be explained, He can only be exalted. He cannot be analyzed, only adored. He is completely separate and *other* than anything else, and in that separation is His holiness.

When we say "Thou art holy," we are saying that God is "separate" or other than we are. We are saying that God cannot be explained or understood, only worshiped and adored.

We must realize that God is totally separate from us. We cannot be sanctified, holy and separate until we get the revelation in our spirits of His holiness. We cannot drag God down to the level of humanity, but we must separate ourselves from sin and allow the Holy Spirit to lift us up to His glory.

In the Old Testament temple, the glory and presence of God was confined behind a thick veil. But that veil was torn down the middle when Jesus died on the cross, signifying that the way was now open for God to tabernacle or dwell in the hearts of believers.

However, we still must separate ourselves from the world and sin to come into His presence. The cleansing blood of Jesus is available to all men, but that blood must be received and applied to our hearts by faith. There must be a genuine repentance and hatred for all sin and uncleanness.

Job said that when he considered the Lord he trembled and feared Him. (Job 23:15.) Much of the Church today does not fear God. Many have an ungodly arrogance born out of a gospel of humanism, that exalts the creature over the creator. But God is *holy*! He is *other* than we are. Through

Him we are made pure because He *is* purity. Through Him we are made holy, because He is perfect holiness.

The Church, in large measure, has traded boldness for arrogance and piety for pride, and instead of boldly yet humbly approaching the throne of *grace*, we arrogantly demand our ''rights.'' God says that pride comes before a fall. James tells us that God resists the proud but gives grace to the humble. (James 4:6.)

I am talking about the secrets of the heart. What is the *motive* of your heart? Are you more concerned with *your* agenda than God's? Have *you* been to the cross, *personally*? Has *your* will been crucified so *His* will can reign supreme? Are you sanctified — *set apart* for the Master's use?

That's what godly holiness is all about — a heart transplant, not external actions and appearances we can use to compare ourselves to one another. Holiness is a matter of the *heart* — a heart that is pure before God; a heart that places the will of God ahead of our will; a heart that willingly lays down its life for the purposes of God in the earth.

Holiness, or sanctification, *must* be the starting point. Without it, we cannot even see the Lord, much less commune with Him, know His will and receive of His goodness. We must come to the cross *ourselves*. Our preaching must bring sinners to *repentance* — not a change of mind that decides to join a church or fellowship, but true *repentance* — a *heart change* that turns in revulsion from sin and embraces the holiness and righteousness of Jesus. That is the preaching which will snatch men from hell and set them on the road to victorious, Spirit-led living in the kingdom of God.

HOLINESS BRINGS THE ANOINTING

3

Holiness Brings the Anointing

**And it shall come to pass in that day, that his
burden shall be taken away from off thy shoulder, and
his yoke from off thy neck, and the yoke shall be
destroyed because of the anointing.**

Isaiah 10:27

I believe God is raising up ministers and preachers of
righteousness in these last days — men and women who
will be forerunners of the second coming of Christ. They
will cry out against sin, prepare the way of the Lord and
make His paths straight. God is raising up powerful
ministers who will move in the anointing of God and
destroy the yokes of bondage off the people.

If these are the last days, and we are going out in the
power of the Spirit as Jesus did, then our message should
be the same as his message. John the Baptist started off with
that word we don't like to hear — *repent!* (Matt. 4:17; Mark
1:15.) Why? Because the kingdom of God is at hand.

In these last days, preachers won't just tickle itching
ears by telling people what they want to hear, but they will
say, "Thus saith the Lord," whether the congregation likes
it or not.

Luke 4:18 tells us Jesus walked into the synagogue,
picked up the book of Isaiah, and began to read, **The Spirit
of the Lord is upon me, because he hath anointed me to
preach the gospel to the poor.**

In the Scriptural context, "anointed" means to be
consecrated — separated, sanctified, holy. Jesus knew that

27

His power, and our power, is in separation from the world. If we want to destroy every yoke of the enemy with the anointing of the Holy Spirit, then we must be separated, sanctified and holy unto God.

We want to be blessed — so blessed we can't contain it. Many Christians equate blessing with finances, big churches and material goods. But I am not so sure about that. Often when Jesus preached, the crowds left. They came by the droves to get healed, and to get the loaves and fishes. But when Jesus started preaching the *truth* about Himself, as in John 6:32-65, most of His disciples left Him. (John 6:66.)

This is not a popular message, but it is a *powerful* message. There is *power* in separation from the world. There is power in sanctification. That is what gives God His power — He is completely separate, completely "other." There is none like Him.

If we want His power and anointing, we must separate ourselves from the world. It is time for the Church to quit blending into the world — to quit warming ourselves by the fire of the world. The world cannot satisfy the sons of God, and it will drain us of our power and anointing. We can never be satisfied with the flickering flames of the world — only the blazing fire of the Holy Ghost burning in our souls will ever satisfy us.

Do we *really* want the blessings of *God* the way He gives them? If so, we need to look again at the words of Jesus in Matthew 5:3-12. Those who Jesus calls *blessed* are the "poor in spirit," they that "mourn," the "meek," the "merciful," and the "pure in heart," among others. He finishes the list with what we don't like to hear in verse 11, **Blessed are ye, when men shall revile you, and persecute you, and shall say all manner of evil against you falsely, for my sake.**

When Jesus walked into the synagogue and read from Isaiah that the Spirit of the Lord was upon Him, the Jews were so incensed that they grabbed Him and carried Him out to a cliff to kill Him. Jesus came *confronting* the powers of darkness, and some of the worst of those demons were in the religious leaders of the day.

It is no different today. Those who will separate themselves from the world, and preach the Gospel without compromise, *will* suffer persecution. But Jesus said that is the way to be truly *blessed!*

God is calling men and women today who will separate themselves from this world and its systems and live holy, sanctified, separated lives — lives that will be fit vessels to carry the anointing and power of the Holy Ghost that will break the yokes of bondage and set the captives free!

Only the Anointing Destroys the Yoke

Is not this the fast that I have chosen? to loose the bands of wickedness, to undo the heavy burdens, and to let the oppressed go free, and that ye break every yoke?

Isaiah 58:6

. . .and the yoke shall be destroyed because of the anointing.

Isaiah 10:27

Are we really interested in breaking every yoke? If we are, then we must understand that there is only *one* thing that breaks and destroys the yoke of bondage from the enemy — the anointing of God!

That anointing we have is from God and abides within us. The anointing is the perpetual propulsion of the power of God which will propel us through every line of Satan's defense.

Satan tries to build walls to keep us away from the blessings of God. He wants to build a wall and refortify the wall and keep us bound up and blind to our inheritance. The *only* thing that will tear down the walls Satan has erected is the *anointing*.

It is not the applause of men that will break yokes — nor the accolades of the news media. Yokes will not be broken because we go to the right church and the pastor is superpowered or the program is always new. Yokes are not destroyed because we know the three faith foundations or confess all the right scriptures.

The Anointing Comes Through Holiness

There is only *one* thing that destroys the yoke — the *anointing* of Almighty God! This anointing is absolutely and entirely about consecration and separation — it has to do with *holiness!*

We don't hear much preaching on holiness. We are told to pray long, to pray loud, to confess more, to believe more — but none of those things *alone* will destroy the yoke of bondage from people. Isaiah 10:27 says the yoke will be destroyed for *one reason* — because of the *anointing!*

Let us once again seek the face of God that His presence would overwhelm our lives. We don't need the *power* — we need the *presence* of God. If we have His *presence*, we will be overwhelmed with His *power*. Where God's presence abides, His power abides.

We *have* that presence! We *have* that anointing. First John 2:20 says that we have an unction, or anointing, from the Holy One. Verse 27 of the same chapter says, **the anointing that ye have received of him abideth in you ... but as the same anointing teacheth you of all things, and is truth, and is no lie....**

The way we get and keep the anointing that destroys the yoke is by being separated — consecrated — *sanctified!* We can grieve the Holy Spirit (Eph. 4:30) and cause His presence and anointing to lift from us. To avoid that, we must constantly separate ourselves from uncleanness and unrighteousness in thought, word or action. We must be *sanctified, set apart, holy* unto Him.

We don't like to hear messages about sanctification. It conjures up an image in our minds of someone who looks like he was baptized in pickle juice, who lived upside down in a post hole, and just bounced off the back of a covered wagon! We think of outward rules and regulations — make sure your dress is this long, your sleeves are so long, and your hair is styled a certain way.

But those external measurements are not sanctification! Sanctification is *separation* — it is *consecration!* It is a bringing out, a cutting loose and a joining unto.

Positional Sanctification

Sanctification begins when we are born again. God **...hath delivered us from the power of darkness, and hath translated us into the kingdom of his dear Son** (Col. 1:13). When we were born again, we became *positionally* sanctified. As far as God is concerned, we have left the kingdom of darkness and have been translated into the kingdom of light.

The problem is, while we are *positionally* sanctified and separated, in our born-again spirit, we must still bring our soul and body into agreement. Throughout his epistles, Paul constantly admonished his readers to separate themselves from the world — to stop living after the old manner of life. He contrasted the works of the flesh and the fruit of the Spirit in Galatians 5:16-26. In Romans 6:1 he emphatically stated that the grace of God is *not* a license to continue in sin. The major reason for writing First Corinthians was to deal with sin in the Church. Paul knew better than anyone that just because we are *positionally* sanctified does not mean we can live any way we feel like and still experience the anointing of God.

Experiential Sanctification

When we are born again, we get *positionally* sanctified. As we live the new life in Christ, we get *experientially* sanctified. When we are *positionally* sanctified, God takes us out of the world. But when we are *experientially* sanctified, God takes the world out of us!

We don't hear this preached much today because some people think it is legalism and bondage. But it is not bondage to live right — it is ultimate freedom! People who flee fornication and promiscuous sex don't have to worry about sexually transmitted diseases. People who carry on their business and financial affairs with honesty and integrity don't have to worry about being arrested for fraud or tax evasion. When we renew our minds with the Word of God and separate ourselves from the unrighteous works of darkness — *experiential sanctification* — then we can walk in the freedom and peace that comes from communion with God and the anointing of God that destroys every yoke.

Ultimate Sanctification

Finally, there is *ultimate sanctification. Ultimate sanctification* is the sanctification of our bodies. *Positional* sanctification deals with the spirit man, when we are born again. *Experiential* sanctification deals with the soul — the mind, will and emotions. But *ultimate* sanctification is spoken of in 1 Corinthians 15:51-58, where Paul says that this corruptible, mortal body shall put on incorruption and immortality. It is spoken of again in 1 Thessalonians 4:16, 17:

> **For the Lord himself shall descend from heaven with a shout, with the voice of the archangel, and with the trump of God: and the dead in Christ shall rise first:**
>
> **Then we which are alive and remain shall be caught up together with them in the clouds, to meet the Lord in the air: and so shall we ever be with the Lord.**

We are going to be changed in a moment, in the twinkling of an eye. We will be consecrated, set apart in our *bodies*. We will be *ultimately sanctified!*

Power Comes From Holiness

The power of God, the unction of God, the anointing of God is wrapped up in the *holiness* of God. God has power because He is *separate* from sin. We have power because we are separate from sin and the world.

When we are born again, we enter a new realm of power. God said in John 14:13, 14 that when we ask anything in His name He will do it. In Luke 9:1 Jesus gave us power and authority over *all* devils and to cure diseases.

We have power and authority with God, but that power comes from separation from sin. That power comes from sanctification — *experiential sanctification* — when we *choose* to separate ourselves and walk a holy and godly life in reverence and awe. *Holy living* — not outward show of dress or manner of prayer — is what will separate us unto God and allow His power to flow through us to break every yoke.

THE SAMSON
SYNDROME

4

The Samson Syndrome

And when Delilah saw that he had told her all his heart, she sent and called for the lords of the Philistines, saying, Come up this once, for he hath shewed me all his heart. Then the Lords of the Philistines came up unto her, and brought money in their hand.

And she said, The Philistines be upon thee, Samson. And he awoke out of his sleep, and said, I will go out as at other times before, and shake myself. *And he wist not that the Lord was departed from him.*

Judges 16:18, 20

This is one of the saddest passages in the Bible. Samson had become so complacent that he believed he could do whatever he wanted and keep the anointing of God. Repeated attempts to trick his secret out of him did not make him repent and separate himself to God.

Instead, he became more arrogant. He went from one seductive woman to another, satisfying his lusts, thinking that the anointing would never leave him. Finally, he came to Delilah, who was too much for him. His defenses were worn down and he gave away the secret of his great strength.

Samson is a type of the Church. Many have put their head in the lap of Delilah, thinking they can always get up one more time and shake off the enemy. They think the anointing will never leave them, no matter how they compromise with the world. Like Samson, many in the

Church do not even know the anointing has left until it is too late, and they are captured by the enemy.

Samson had *power.* He walked up to Philistine cities, picked up the city gates off their hinges and carried them on his back. He killed thousands of the enemy with the jawbone of an ass, and nothing they could devise would stop him or hold him prisoner.

Samson was a man of God, full of strength, power and anointing. He could destroy the yoke. But Samson started going where he shouldn't go and hearing what he shouldn't hear, and seeing what he shouldn't see — then he started doing what he shouldn't do.

Many in the Church are caught up in the Samson syndrome. We have preachers that would make better Hollywood and Wall Street moguls than preachers. Many preachers would make better businessmen, because that is what their mind is on all the time. Many would be better Hollywood superstars than preachers, because ninety percent of what they do is an act!

There's Something Wrong in the Church

There's something *wrong* in the Church when teenagers can commit fornication on Friday night and then come into the sanctuary on Sunday morning, lift their hands and dance before the Lord.

There's something *wrong* when we command deafness to go and it doesn't go. Jesus said in Luke 9:1 that He has given us power over *all* devils and to cure diseases. There is something *wrong* when we pray for the sick and they do not recover.

There is something *wrong* when there is no convicting power of the Holy Ghost in our services, and the altars in our meeting places are as barren as the womb of a 100-year-old woman. *No generation in history has talked more about revival and experienced less of it than this one.*

No generation could talk about having so much when it actually possessed so little unless it had been so far separated from a move of God that it could not even recognize when it didn't have one. It is the Samson syndrome — *we are not even aware that the Spirit of God is gone.*

It is time the Church took her head out of the lap of Delilah and stopped trying to look, think and act like the world. It is time for the music in the Church to stop imitating the music in the world.

We need music with *anointing!* We need preaching with *unction!* It is time we began to see our altars full of sinners crying out in true repentance for mercy on their lost souls. It is time for our communities to *change* — to be rid of pornography, abortion, violence and crime.

I want a move of God! I long for a *real* move of God where the altars are filled with Christians, weeping for the anointing of God in their lives. I long to see born-again, blood washed saints crying from the depths of their hearts along with David in Psalm 51:1, 10, 11:

> **Have mercy upon me, O God, according to thy lovingkindness: according unto the multitude of thy tender mercies blot out my transgressions ... Create in me a clean heart, O God; and renew a right spirit within me. Cast me not away from thy presence; and take not thy holy spirit from me.**

We are so self-satisfied and so self-indulgent. We have filled ourselves and become drunk on the wine of the humanistic gospel. We talk about who *we* are and what *we* have accomplished. But we've forgotten about the world outside our sanctuary walls that is doomed, desperate, and diseased. We've forgotten about suffering, sighing, crying, dying humanity. We've made our focus ourselves and what *we* want from the throne of God.

It is time for the Church of Jesus Christ to wash her robes white in the blood of the Lamb — to come out from among them and be separate, for in that separation there is power. We need a remnant people that will stop asking how close to the world they can get and still be in the kingdom. *We need a Church that will ask how far into the kingdom they can get and still be on this earth!*

We need a people that so hunger and thirst after the presence of God that they will not even realize when their television has been off for six months, because they are so consumed with the fire and passion of a holy God.

We must become so totally consumed with Him that we will not be satisfied until His presence is with us continually — until we look at every person and see Christ and become brokenhearted with our own spiritual bankruptcy. *The Church in America must repent of its glamorous idolatry and its spiritual adultery!* We have left our first love. We worship at the altar of self-indulgent pleasure.

The Goodness of God Leads to Repentance

This is not a negative message. It is not a call to do this and don't do something else. I'm talking about getting so excited about what God is doing that we don't *want* what the world has to offer. Romans 2:4 says it is the *goodness* of God that leads to repentance. That means when God shows us a steak dinner, we look at the mess we are eating and decide we would rather have the steak. We see what God is offering, and we leave the world and its passions and lusts behind. We count all things but dung for the excellency of Christ, that we might win Him. (Phil. 3:8.)

Sin Is Not Accidental

Nobody *falls* into sin. Sin is *planned!* First Corinthians 10:13 says that God will not allow us to be tempted beyond what we can bear, but with every temptation will *make a way of escape.* We don't *have* to commit adultery or

38

fornication. *We can run!* Joseph was chased by Potiphar's wife, and he went to prison for not compromising.

Yet we have preachers that fall into adultery and say, "I'm just weak in the flesh." That is absolutely the point — we *are* weak in the flesh. But Paul told us in Romans 7 and 8 how to overcome. He was weak in the flesh also, but he was *strong in the Spirit!* The next time temptation knocks at the door, why not pray in tongues and let the Holy Ghost answer?

Repentance Is More Than an Apology

When we do sin, many just come to the altar and apologize. *We have reduced repentance to an apology!* But God does not want our apology! He wants true repentance — a *change* of heart that will *stop* the sin! He wants us to rend our hearts and not our garments. He wants us to realize that sin separates us from His holy presence. When we are separated, there is no fellowship, no power, no *life!*

Without God's Presence There Is No Judgment of Sin

The presence of God departed means judgment delayed. When we see the judgment of God coming it is time to rejoice, because His presence is there!

In the interest of scriptural accuracy, I want to clarify what I mean by the term "presence of God" as used in this book.

Since earliest childhood, we have been taught that one of the cardinal attributes of God is that He is omnipresent, or always present. We also have the words of Jesus found in Hebrews 13:15. **. . . I will never leave thee, nor forsake thee.** In light of these truths, the reader might wonder how I can reconcile the statement, "God's presence departed means judgment delayed."

The presence of God is twofold. It is the difference between a cloudy day and a sunny day. Both have the presence of light, but only one has the brilliance. Kings in ancient days at the gate of the city or palace dispensed judgment. In their court, they dispensed favor. Only those intimate with the king or those especially invited were welcome. At both the gate of judgment and the court of intimacy, one could be said to be in the "presence" of the monarch. But only those to whom he had extended the royal scepter in welcome experienced his glorious favor. (Esther 4:16.)

The children of Israel in the wilderness all experienced the presence of God, but only Moses experienced the full glory. In these last days, God is taking away the clouds and the veil, and His glory is beginning to break forth. His glorious presence will do today what it has always done — it will annihilate uncovered sin.

Thanks be to God, the Christian can experience the sanctifying daily cleansing of the blood of Jesus, but only if we walk in the full light of God's Word.

Isaiah 26:9 says:

> **With my soul have I desired thee in the night; yea, with my spirit within me will I seek thee early:** *for when thy judgments are in the earth, the inhabitants of the world will learn righteousness.*

The righteous judgments of God are *desirable* to those who belong to Him. For, as Isaiah says, it is only when His judgments are in the earth that we learn righteousness. Sin separates man from God, and His judgment on sin separates man from sin and directs him back to God again. For the saints of God, judgment is not to be feared and avoided, but welcomed and embraced. Let us cry out in the night that His judgments be in the earth, that all that offends Him and cuts off our fellowship with Him be exposed and removed, whether it be in our individual lives, the corporate Body of Christ or the society in which we live.

We have emphasized righteousness consciousness so strongly that we have almost forgotten to preach holiness. *Righteousness* is what God does for us. It is a *free gift*, imparted by God, and cannot be earned or purchased. (Rom. 4:3-8.)

Holiness is concerned with *our* response to God. First Peter 1:16 *commands* us, ...**Be ye holy; for I am holy.** God *imparts* righteousness to us, but we *choose* to separate ourselves, to consecrate ourselves and walk holy before Him.

Holiness Requires Change

If we truly want to walk in holiness, we must be willing to change. We can sing and dance and shout. We can get goose bumps and good feelings, but is there any *real change?*

Change is important, because the byproduct of God changing us is the manifestation of His presence in our midst. His presence is His glory, and He is changing us from glory to glory as we behold His face. (2 Cor. 3:18.) When we let God change us, He takes us to new levels of manifestation of His presence in our life. Then we don't have to run from preacher to preacher to get a "touch" from God — His anointing will rise up within us and manifest His presence.

Conviction Brings Repentance

True repentance comes when we allow the Holy Ghost to convict us of sin. After Samson laid his head in the lap of Delilah and lost his anointing, he was captured, his eyes were gouged out and he was put in prison. But his fall from power destroyed his pride, and God was able to convict him and lead him to repentance and humility. The final anointing God placed on him allowed him to kill more Philistines in his death than he did in his entire life. (Judg. 16:30.)

Even though he repeatedly sinned and lost his anointing and ministry, Samson repented and returned to God and gained a mention in "faith's hall of fame." (Heb. 11:32.)

Repentance is a good thing. When we are on our knees repenting, His presence comes to consume the sacrifice of a repentant heart before Him. His presence fills our life and His power overflows.

But we cannot have true repentance without conviction! We have been so busy pulling in the net that we forgot to sort out the fish. One minister suggested that as the end of the age approaches, we ought to build a twelve-foot-high fence around our altars and put barbed wire on the top of it and see who tries to scale the fence. Then we will know who *really* wants to get out of the kingdom of darkness and into the kingdom of light. We would know who has *really* repented and who would rather have God or die!

The Church Must Repent

It is not just the lost who need to repent. Christians must also repent. We need to repent of coldheartedness. We need to repent that we don't care more about getting our neighbor's needs met than we do our own. We need to repent that we never have to stop what we are doing because the glory and presence of God has so overwhelmed us we cannot carry on with our normal routine!

God will not dwell where there is sin, but if we will separate ourselves unto Him, He will flood our lives like a torrent and His presence will envelop us like a garment.

We can sip our wine, listen to off-color jokes and snuggle up to the world, but it will cost us the presence of God. Then there will come a time when the Philistines will come on us. *Our enemy will come.* It may be cancer in our body, a demon spirit sent to torment our mind or an adulterous relationship.

It doesn't matter where it comes from — if we have our head in the lap of Delilah when our Philistine enemy comes, we will be as defeated as Samson. We may think we can jump up and shake off the enemy just like we always have, but one day we will wake up and find the anointing is gone — the power of God has left — and we are carried off captive to our enemies.

Let us hear the cry of God's heart today for a people who will separate themselves from the world and its ways and walk holy, sanctified and set apart to Him. God is looking for a people who will renounce the world and run under the arm of God, to get as close to God as we possibly can.

God is calling for a people who will rebuke every temptation and walk in total victory in the presence of a holy God. Such a people will have His power without measure to change the world, because they have His Spirit without measure.

DON'T FORGET THE CROSS

5
Don't Forget the Cross

We are troubled on every side, yet not distressed; we are perplexed, but not in despair;

Persecuted, but not forsaken; cast down, but not destroyed;

Always bearing about in the body the dying of the Lord Jesus, that the life also of Jesus might be made manifest in our body.

For we which live are alway delivered unto death for Jesus' sake, that the life also of Jesus might be made manifest in our mortal flesh.

2 Corinthians 4:8-11

To talk about holiness is to talk about the cross. Paul wrote the Church at Corinth in 1 Corinthians 2:2 that he **...determined not to know anything among you, save Jesus Christ, and him crucified.**

He wrote to the Church at Galatia (Gal. 2:20) and said, **I am crucified with Christ: nevertheless I live; yet not I, but Christ liveth in me.** Later in the same book (Gal. 5:24) he says, **And they that are Christ's have crucified the flesh with the affections and lusts.**

In Philippians 3:10,11 (AMP), Paul states:

[For my determined purpose is] that I may know Him — that I may progressively become more deeply and intimately acquainted with Him, perceiving and recognizing and understanding [the wonders of His Person] more strongly and more clearly. And that I may in that same way come to know the power outflowing from His resurrection [which it exerts over believers];

45

**and that I may so share His sufferings as to be
continually transformed [in spirit into his likeness
even] to His death, [in the hope]**

   **That if possible I may attain to the [spiritual and
moral] resurrection [that lifts me] out from among the
dead [even while in the body].**

The Cross Is Ultimate Sanctification

The death of Jesus on the cross was the ultimate act
of sanctification. In that act, Jesus made the final and eternal
sacrifice for sin, and broke forever the power hold of Satan
over man.

Our salvation comes through faith in Him — through
believing in what He did on the cross and in the resurrection
from the grave. When a person hears about Jesus and
believes, he is freely given eternal life. He is born again of
the Spirit, and passes from death into life.

But salvation in this present life is an ongoing process.
Paul preached the *cross* throughout his letters to the
Churches. He sought to be conformed to the *death* of Jesus
that the *life* of Jesus could be manifested in him. The Church
needs this message today. We need to have the *cross* burned
on our hearts; we need to be constantly living as ones who
are dead, dead to the world and its lusts, that we might
be alive to the resurrection power of Jesus!

Decision Without Conversion

William Booth, the founder of the Salvation Army, once
said, ''The problem in the Twentieth Century church will
be that they have decision without conversion, and they
have conversion without lordship. They will have a message
of heaven without hell and grace without judgment. They
will change the truth of God into a lie.''

For many years we have had a gospel of humanism
perpetrated on us wherein we have attempted to bring God

down to our level by exalting ourselves up to God's level. We have become the king of our own kingdom and used the Bible to dress up the lustful, idolatrous desires of our generation with spiritual garments to get us into a position that the world calls success, because we believe that is life.

In many cases, the Church has bought a lie. We have been told that gold would satisfy, that luxury cars would satisfy, that looking like a magazine model would satisfy. To a large extent, the Church has bought the success image of the world. We have tried to use the Bible to get anything we want from God. We dress it up in spiritual terms and call it life.

But Jesus said that if we want to find our life, we must first lose it. (Matt. 10:39.) In the verse preceding that He said, **And he that taketh not his cross, and followeth after me, is not worthy of me.**

God Cannot Be Manipulated

Many have begun to take the Word of God and manipulate it to the point that they think they can tell God what is right and wrong for them! That has been the deception of the devil from the Garden of Eden to the present. In Romans 1:22-25, Paul talks about people who exchanged the glory of God for their own lifestyle, and worshiped the creature instead of the Creator.

Sadly enough, much of the Church has done the same thing — especially in America. Some have perverted the Gospel of the goodness of God and His desire to bless and prosper His children and twisted it into a gospel of success that pampers the flesh and denies suffering or tribulation. Yet Jesus clearly told His disciples in John 16:33, **...In the world ye *shall have* tribulation: but *be of good cheer; I have overcome the world.***

Jesus never said we would not suffer persecution or tribulation. He just said to rejoice in it because in Him we have the victory over it. The problem is, we think that anything that distresses our flesh or takes away our "creature comforts" is of the devil. *We have missed the cross!*

The Disciples of Jesus Will Take Up the Cross

Jesus said that those who would be His disciples must take up their *cross* and follow Him. A cross is only good for one thing — *death!* A cross is not a pogo stick, and it is not a ladder. It is *death.*

Many think life is pleasure to the flesh. They look at big homes, fancy cars, jewelry, and beautiful bodies and say, "This is *living!*" But that is not *life.* That is a lie of the devil. A person can have all the pleasures of the world and be so miserably sick in their soul they wish they could die.

The cross Jesus calls us to bear is a death to self and selfish pleasures. It is coming to a place that we have pleasure in *nothing* the world offers, and He becomes *everything.* He wants to be our all-in-all, our substance, our joy, our supply, our strength, our power and our vision.

Kingdom Life Is Different From the World

Jesus talked about kingdom life. Kingdom life is different from what the world portrays as life. Kingdom life can be confusing, because Jesus said if we want to *live* we have to *die.* If we want to *get,* we have to *give.* The only way up is down. Everything in the kingdom of God is diametrically opposed to what the world calls life.

Kingdom life is *separation* from the world. It is a walk in *holiness* and *sanctification.* Kingdom life is life in the presence of the Holy One — life in the presence of the King. Kingdom life is life in surrender — *living through dying!* It is being exalted by being humble.

Taking up our cross does not mean that God does not want to bless and prosper us. But before the resurrection can come, the death must first come. Before God can pour out Himself on us, we must leave all and follow Him.

God desires to have us more than we can possibly desire to lay hold on Him. We were created for His pleasure, not the other way around. But all too often, we go to the altar and give our life to God and then ask what *we* are going to get in exchange.

We need to get to the point where we are not just looking for exchange, but we are looking for change! We need to get to the point where the burden of our sin has gone so far over our head that we can no longer tolerate it or lift our head above it — where all we can do is cry out as Paul did in Romans 7:24, **O wretched man that I am! who shall deliver me from the body of this death?**

All Paul was interested in was to get the spirit of the age off of himself and come into the resurrection life of Jesus — the life in the spirit.

Jesus did not tell us to take His Word and learn to use it to manipulate God into giving us whatever our flesh wants. He said things like, "take no thought for tomorrow, what you shall eat or what you shall wear." He said to seek *first* the kingdom of God and His righteousness, and all these things we need will be added to us. (Matt. 6:25-34.)

God Wants Us More Than We Want Him

If we ever doubt that God wants to give us abundant life more than we want to get it, we have only to look at His cross compared to ours. What did He give up to reach us compared to what we give up to know Him? There is no comparison. God wants to give it *all* to us, but it will only come through the cross. It will only come as we are willing to die to *our* plans, desires and wants and seek what *He* wants for us, *no matter what the cost.*

But that is not the way we usually operate in the American church of today. If we don't get the job we want, we give up and think God has fallen off the throne. We complain that we have prayed for six weeks and confessed it until we thought our tongue would fall out. We figure out every possible reason why our believing and confessing and praying did not work except the obvious one — *it was not in God's plan for us to have that specific job.* There is a vital ingredient we have left out. It is called *sovereignty!*

A minister may cry out to God, ''God, I want to pastor 5,000 people. I confess with my mouth that I'm going to pastor 5,000!'' God may be telling that minister to go pastor 50, and the man is insisting on pastoring 5,000. That is treachery to God. *He* is the King in this kingdom, not us!

Confession is a valid principle, *when the will of God is known.* But there is no Bible verse to tell a minister what his specific ministry is or what size church he should pastor. That has to be received from the Spirit of God. Once God has spoken, then confession is a valid, scriptural principle. But all too often, we get the cart before the horse and decide what *we* want and try to confess it into existence.

Some have made themselves gods! They have exalted a gospel of pure humanism, telling God, the Sovereign Monarch of this kingdom, what they will and will not do. They try to use God's Word as some kind of a stave to get God positioned to where they want Him.

God Is Sovereign

The Church today needs a revelation of the sovereignty of God. We need to remember that Jesus said the greatest among us is the servant of all. (Matt. 20:27.)

When we get a revelation of the sovereignty of God, we will change our faith confessions to confessing we are servants — confessing we are taking up our cross and dying to self that the life of Jesus be manifested in us. We would stop running around telling everyone what our ''gift'' is.

Our "gift" would be our life, submitted to God to be used for His glory.

This has nothing to do with physical infirmity. Physical infirmity was dealt with at the cross, and the Word and will of God is clear. He purchased our healing by His stripes, and we have a covenant right to believe it, confess it and be healed. (Matt. 8:17; 1 Pet. 2:24.)

What we *don't* have a covenant right to is the gratification of our flesh. We tell sinners to come to the altar and confess they have made a mess of their lives, but we also need altar calls for Christians to confess they have misused the principles of God and tried to tell Him what to do.

The mature believer will come to the place that Shadrach, Meschach and Aabednego did. (Dan. 3:16-18.) When Nebuchadnezzar threatened to throw them in the fiery furnace if they did not worship his idol, they told him, "Go ahead; our God will deliver us, *but if not*, we still won't bow to your gods."

Faith is the pledging of our fidelity, *no matter what the results.* What many Christians today have done is pervert the message of John 10:10, where Jesus says,

> **The thief cometh not, but for to steal, and to kill, and to destroy: I am come that they might have life, and that they might have it more abundantly.**

Many have made neat little cliche formulas, and wanted to put anything that hurts our flesh over on the side of the thief, or devil, and everything that pleasures our flesh on the "life" or God side. But Jesus taught that the way to "life" was *death* — death to self, death to the flesh and death to our own plans and desires.

God calls us to deny ourselves, take no thought for tomorrow, and acknowledge Him in all our ways, that *He* might direct our path. (Prov. 3:6.)

Abandonment to God Acknowledges Sovereignty

In abandonment to God, the mature believer proclaims, from a consecrated life, that everything in his life is either the perfect and sovereign will of God, or else God, *in His sovereignty*, allowed it into his life — or we, as believers, have opened the door to the enemy by letting down our shield of faith through ignorance or perhaps even sin. When tests, trials, tribulations or problems that bring discomfort to the flesh come, and we stand on the Word, we allow the tests and trials to conform us to the *death* of Jesus so that we can then be conformed to the image of His resurrection.

All too often we get hung up on words and definitions. When something bad happens, we wonder, ''Is this God or the devil?'' We assume that anything that makes our flesh uncomfortable is automatically the devil.

Some have even suggested that the apostle Paul needed to have ''our Twentieth Century'' revelation. But if Paul had ''our'' revelation, he probably would not have written two-thirds of the New Testament. Much of what we call ''revelation'' is nothing more than manipulation, trying to make God do what we want to keep our flesh comfortable.

God is not a mean God Who afflicts and punishes His children. But we have an enemy who opposes the work of God in the earth and will do anything to stop God's Church from completing its mission in the earth. We can either fight the circumstances in our lives and try to *manipulate* God to get us out of uncomfortable situations, or we can *submit* to God and *trust* Him to take us *through* the fire to *His* victory.

We Don't Have To Stay Defeated

No matter what happens in our lives, we don't have to put up with it. We can face adverse circumstances and deny their right to remain in our lives. But God is not as interested in the circumstances that come into our lives as He is in the way we *respond* to those circumstances.

If a little tribulation comes into our life, are we ready to throw down the Bible and quit? This is where true spiritual warfare comes in. *Can we resist the pressure to stop serving God when things are not comfortable?* Can we submit to God in *every* circumstance and say, ''God, I don't believe this came from you, and I am going to resist the enemy attack. But meanwhile, I will let these circumstances make me more like You. I will refuse to murmur and complain. I will refuse to doubt Your faithfulness or curse the people who wronged me. I will love and not hate. I will forgive, when I have been wronged.''

Such a response will build *character* in us and allow God to form the image of His Son in us. We need to get out of our baby stage, where we nurse the hurts and question why God would allow the devil to do such a thing in our life. We need to realize that God is faithful, that He *always* wants the best for us, and that He pursues us more than we pursue Him.

God Wants Us To Pursue Him

At times when God seems distant from us, He wants us to pursue Him more. He is a jealous God, and He will stand back at times and say, ''Do you want Me or not?'' The real test of our hearts before God is when we can withstand any adversity, any temptation, any circumstance the devil throws at us and remain faithful to God, *whether we are instantly delivered or not!*

James admonishes us in James 1:2-4:

> **My brethren, count it all joy when ye fall into divers temptations;**
>
> **Knowing this, that the trying of your faith worketh patience.**
>
> **But let patience have her perfect work, that ye may be perfect and entire, wanting nothing.**

When the devil throws problems and tragedy in our path, we gain the victory when we submit to God, resist the devil and count it all joy. Joseph tried to get away from Potiphar's wife. He did everything right, walked in purity and integrity, and ended up in jail. He could have cried and murmured and accused God of unfaithfulness, or tried to manipulate God to get him released. But he chose to submit to God, even when he could not understand the reason for his circumstances. When Joseph trusted God and submitted to God in the prison *for years,* God was able to do a deep work in Joseph and prepare him to be Prime Minister of Egypt.

Sacrifice in the American Church Today

Much of the Body of Christ in the United States of America knows nothing of sacrifice. We think it is a sacrifice to make $1,000 and give God $100, when the tithe belonged to God all along!

The Church needs to grow up and realize that the kingdom of God does not come to us just because we went to an altar one day and decided to be a nice person. It comes when we surrender to Jesus as *Lord* and let Him bring real *change* in our life.

We often want all the blessings of God and none of the sacrifice. Jesus came to earth knowing that His end and purpose was death. Today He calls His Church to take up the cross and follow Him — the cross that denies our own life and lays down everything dear and important to us to follow Him.

We must learn to count it all joy. If the devil can't steal our joy, he can't keep our goods. The way to exaltation in the kingdom of God is through servanthood. The way to life is death to self. The way to get is to give. The way to success with God is always through the cross.

SPIRITUAL WARFARE REQUIRES HOLINESS

6

Spiritual Warfare Requires Holiness

To the intent that now unto the principalities and powers in heavenly places might be known by the church the manifold wisdom of God,

According to the eternal purpose which he purposed in Christ Jesus our Lord.

Ephesians 3:10, 11

Put on the whole armour of God, that ye may be able to stand against the wiles of the devil.

For we wrestle not against flesh and blood, but against principalities, against powers, against the rulers of the darkness of this world, against spiritual wickedness in high places.

Ephesians 6:11, 12

We are involved in a battle! If anyone says otherwise, they are not telling the truth! But we are not called to win the battle, because it has already been won for us by Jesus. He has triumphed over all of hell (Col. 2:15) and made a show of them openly. We are called to enforce and maintain Satan's defeat. He has no more authority, and we are commissioned to go forth and tell the world that they are free from prison. Jesus won the victory for them.

The real spiritual warfare comes from the battleground of the mind when the enemy tries to cut off our communication lines to God by getting us out of prayer, faith, and love and getting us into strife with each other or getting us into some other sin. The battle is to keep our mind renewed.

John tells us in 1 John 3:8: **For this purpose the Son of God was manifested, that he might destroy the works of the devil.** When Jesus died on the cross, He said, **It is finished** (John 19:30). He completed the work for which He was sent to the earth. He became the final, complete and eternal sacrifice for sin, and forever destroyed the authority of Satan in the earth.

Jesus Delegated His Power to the Church

Before leaving the earth, Jesus told His disciples in Matthew 28:18 that *all* power and authority in *heaven and earth* had been given unto *Him.* Then He immediately turned that power over to the disciples — the Church — to execute the judgment He had won on Satan and his demons.

He told His disciples (which includes us) to take the authority and power He had won and go into every nation with the Gospel. It is not *our* authority — it is *His* authority. *We* do not tear down strongholds and pull down principalities — we *humble* ourselves before *Him* and allow Him to use us as instruments of His power to defeat Satan and free the people Satan has held captive.

The Lord Is a Man of War

The time for weak, mediocre, mundane, passive Christianity is over! Exodus 15:3 declares, **The Lord is a man of war: The Lord is his name.** When we behold His face and see His glory, we will *know* Him as a warrior. That warring spirit will be in our spirit, and we won't have to have books, seminars and special music to pump us up and plead with us to be warriors. He *is* a warrior, and when we are in Him and He in us, we will manifest His Spirit without hype or manipulation from man.

The story is told that Smith Wigglesworth walked into a train car and a religious leader saw him, fell out of his seat and cried, ''My God, man, you convict me of my sin!''

Wigglesworth had not been to any spiritual warfare conferences. He hadn't learned how to scream loud and scare the devil because he had a strong *natural* voice. He had simply learned that all he needed to drive off the devil and convict men of their sin was the *presence* of Almighty God. He learned that when the presence of God is manifest, judgment is swift!

We do not really understand spiritual warfare. We have many people running around thinking they are storming the gates of hell and pulling down strongholds. But the *real* spiritual warfare takes place within our hearts and minds. The strongholds the devil has built up are in our own minds. We must begin by renewing our minds with the Word of God and cleansing our hearts with the blood of the Lamb.

Crucify the Flesh

The first stage of spiritual warfare is to crucify the flesh. We cannot presume to take cities, nations or even our own block if we have not *first* cleaned the devil and his works out of our own hearts! We want to pull the devil down from the second heaven, but is he still enthroned in our heart? What about our own greed, selfishness or immorality?

If we are not living holy, sanctified lives, the devil will laugh at us when we try to war against him. We cannot satisfy the desires and lusts of the flesh and expect to have any authority over principalities.

If we do not change our attitudes about personal holiness and sanctification, this generation will go down in history as the generation that talked more about having less than any generation on the face of the earth.

True Spiritual Warfare Brings Results

We will be the generation that boasted more in nothing than any other generation. We scream that we are making war in the heavenlies, pulling down strongholds and taking cities for God. Yet we look around any city and see more pornography, more abortions, more crime and more people on the way to hell than ever before.

Instead of the fires of revival, we see *less* influence for God, less stirring in the hearts of men and less crying out for salvation than ever before.

Who are we fooling? It is only a generation that has never been genuinely touched with a revival from *God* that can boast so much with so little manifestation to show for it.

Spiritual Warfare Is Based on Revelation

Spiritual warfare is not based on our ability to overcome devils. Spiritual warfare is based on renewing the mind and the revelation of our heart, that we understand the orders of our Commander-in-Chief.

There is more to spiritual warfare than screaming at the ceiling. Some of the screaming needs to be on the inside of us. We need to cry out, "O wretched man that I am." We need to cry out in repentance for the spiritual bankruptcy, worldly idolatry and Satanic adultery we have allowed to infiltrate and permeate the Church.

G. Campbell Morgan, the great English preacher, said, "Victory begins with the name of Jesus on our lips, but it is consummated with the nature of Jesus on our heart. He is our strength, and our song; follow Him, crown Him and fight under Him."

The Church must come to recognize that Jesus is the sovereign King of His kingdom. *He* has won the victory over Satan and *all* demons — *all* principalities and powers — and it is our job to *believe* Him and go forth manifesting His presence.

Christlikeness Is the Key

The key to spiritual warfare is Christlikeness. Many boast about great things — pulling down strongholds, casting the devil off his throne, making the devil nervous. Many claim to subdue kingdoms and to have their spiritual armor on. They say, "Look who *we* are! *We* are the mighty warriors."

Yes, God has called us to be warriors! Yes, we are to use the authority of Jesus to overcome the devil and release his captives. But our warfare must be according to the principles of the kingdom. James 4:6 and 7 tells us God *resists* the proud and gives *grace* to the *humble*. James tells us to first *submit* ourselves to God, *then* we can resist the devil and he will flee.

The reason much of our warfare is ineffectual is because we have not first submitted to God! We have not humbled ourselves before Him. We have allowed pride to come in and exalt what *we* have done.

Where Are the Results?

Where is the city shaken to its foundation with a revival that changes the very fabric of society? Where are the meetings started by God that no man can stop because no man started them?

Where is the outpouring of God where the Church gets its heart right before God? Where is the power and conviction of God that would draw sinners in off the street because they couldn't resist the mighty power and presence of God?

That level of power and conviction will not return to the Church until we cry out in repentance ourselves and begin to *want* the presence of God more than *anything* else. That kind of power and presence of God went by the way of the "Microwave Church" — the Church that demands "instant" everything.

We Have Formulas and No Faith

We want the formula to be a great soul winner, or the

set of scriptures for instant healing or prosperity. *We have become a people of formulas and no faith!* Faith is not a complicated word — it is simply *trust.* Faith is nothing more or less than knowing God. Faith is not knowing *about* God, or taking someone else's revelation. Faith is *knowing* God ourselves, *personally.*

We have a message of heaven with no hell, salvation without conversion and conversion without lordship. We have taught people to be soul winners with no tears for the lost. We have taught people the seven steps to get healed, but we have lost the heart of compassion Jesus had for the sick and dying.

We have made a religion where God is unnecessary — where all we need are the right formulas, the right buttons to push, the right scriptures to confess, and we can make God do whatever we want Him to.

God must sit in flaming fury and say, ''I am jealous over a people. Where are the people that will come into My presence and *humble* themselves before me and crown me Lord of all? Where are those people?''

Many Have Not Touched the Heart of God

Many have yet to touch the heart of God concerning spiritual warfare. We have so much surface activity with no real depth. We have yet to fathom the depths of the Creator of the universe.

The Church, in large measure, has a lot of *talk* and little *relationship.* We spend no time communicating with God in prayer. We have become prideful and boastful, thinking we are like the great prayer warriors of the past who shook nations and continents for God.

But the real test is, how Christlike are we? How much victory do we see manifested in our own homes and personal lives? How are husbands at loving their wives as

Christ loved the Church? How are wives at submitting to their husbands as unto the Lord? How are we at being a servant? We want God to supply all *our* needs, but whose needs are *we* supplying?

Deliverance Begins at Home

There is no reason for us to go out and make war in the heavenlies when we are in bondage at home. We cannot be sending people to cast out devils from others when they themselves are bound up with fear, torment, discouragement, depression, lust and greed.

If we expect to be great spiritual warriors that take cities and shake nations for Christ, then we must start at home. We must begin by running the devil out of our lives, our families, our businesses and our churches before we win cities and nations. We must overcome the lust of the flesh, the lust of the eyes and the pride of life in *ourselves* before we can start setting the captives free.

We can't talk about being great intercessors and prayer warriors when we can't control our own appetites. Until we bring our own bodies under control — *stop eating everything in sight* — and bring our gossiping, backbiting, murmuring tongues under submission to the Holy Spirit, we dare not talk about pulling down princes over cities!

God Wants To Build Character

G. Campbell Morgan said, ''The severest of battles of a man's life are fought out in secret in his own individual soul.'' Temptation to evil in its varied forms comes far more subtly to a person when he is alone than when he is with others. *Character is not what we do in public — it is what we do in private, when no one can see.*

We will have no victory in the supernatural sphere until we first overcome the enemies of our own body, our own soul and our own spirit. We will never be able to clean up someone else's front doorstep until we first bare our own soul to God. We must rend our hearts before Him, not our garments.

The battle begins in the secret recesses of our inner life, in the hall of our own imagination, in the chamber of our affections. We have to deal with and overcome the fatal mistake Lucifer made. He said "I will" over and over, until he had attempted to exalt himself over the throne of God, and was cast out forever from God's presence.

We must honestly face and deal with the desires and motivations of our hearts. Although we are sons and daughters of God, we are bondservants and slaves to Jesus Christ, and it is *His* plan, purpose and will we follow. "Our rights" and "our plans" need to be submitted with humility to His will and plan.

The Fiercest Battles Are Fought Alone

It is in our own affections that the battle must first be fought and won. The longest and most strenuous battles are fought in absolute loneliness, with just the individual, God and a Bible. It is there that we come to surrender. It is alone with God and His Word that we lay down our lives and willingly take up our cross and follow Him.

When we are alone with God and brutally honest with Him and ourselves we can say with the Psalmist (Ps. 139:23,24):

Search me, O God, and know my heart: try me, and know my thoughts:

And see if there be any wicked way in me, and lead me in the way everlasting.

We can say to God, "Get me straightened up, and when I am straightened up, I'll be ready to face the hordes of hell for you. I'll be ready to subdue kingdoms for you for it is *only then* that I will manifest Jesus. It is *He* that must be manifested to destroy the works of the devil — not me and some inflated opinion of myself.''

Manifesting the Gifts Requires Cleansing

We have an enemy, and we must fight him with the weapons and strategies given us by our Commander. But we cannot expect to run out and manifest the gifts of the Spirit in an uncleansed temple — that is a *farce.*

God is calling us to clean up our own temple before we wage war on the principalities. He is saying to the Church, *Get rid of the envy, jealousy, heresy, revelling, backbiting, lust for things, lust for people, lust for position and anything else that is a work of the flesh — then the power and authority will be there to set the captives free.*

God Wants To Take Us Through the Fire

God is not interested in delivering us *out of* the fires of adversity and tribulation. He wants to get in the fire with us and deliver us *through* the fire. He wants a people who have gone through the purging fires and come out without the smell of smoke. He wants a people who will be a mighty testimony to *His* delivering power.

True spiritual warfare begins when we allow God to have His way in our lives and we submit to Him and His lordship, no matter what the circumstances. When we realize *God* is sovereign and He wants to crucify the sin nature in our flesh — to *destroy* anything that is not Christlike — we can begin to get serious about spiritual warfare. When we come to understand that we are not God, but a *reflection* of Him, we will understand it is His power working *through* us to will and to do His good pleasure. (Phil. 2:13.)

Yes, we fight! Yes, we are victorious *in Him!* But it must come through personal holiness and sanctification. Our power is in our purity, and our purity can only come through total separation from the world and its lusts, and total surrender and submission to the Lordship of Jesus.

HOLINESS
BRINGS REVIVAL

7

Holiness Brings Revival

And it shall come to pass afterward, that I will pour out my spirit upon all flesh; and your sons and your daughters shall prophesy, your old men shall dream dreams, your young men shall see visions:

And also upon the servants and upon the handmaids in those days will I pour out my spirit.

Joel 2:28, 29

Joel prophesied that revival was coming! Peter stood up on the Day of Pentecost and said the revival Joel had prophesied had begun. Revival started this age, and it will end with even greater revival. The revival that is coming on the earth will make every other revival the world has ever known look like a Sunday School picnic compared to the glory of God that will fall on the face of this earth!

We are in the beginnings of the last great endtime revival, and the Church needs to wake up and see what God is doing in the earth. Walls are falling down and people are hearing the Gospel who never heard it before.

Revival is moving across this land also, and we will never be the same. When there is revival, saints get right with God. When there is revival, the *power* of God is in manifestation. The *authority* of God is resident in His people. Revival will turn *potential* energy — energy at rest — into *kinetic* energy — energy in motion.

Revival Is More Than Numbers

Sadly, there have been many come into the Church because they found a better *lifestyle* than what they were in — but there was no real *conviction* of sin and *repentance* worked out in their life. Because there was not real godly sorrow and repentance, many are not serving God today.

Revival is more than getting numbers on the roll! Revival is not the Charismatic renewal. The Charismatic renewal did not really touch or change society — it just showed the Church some gifts she had from God and wasn't using.

Revival is when the hearts of men burn until they cannot sleep. *Revival* is when men and women of God walk down the street and sinners fall down and repent because of the glory of God manifested in His saints. *Revival* is when we don't have to advertise and hype a meeting, because the Spirit of God is drawing people from every direction. *Revival* is when the presence of God is so strong on His people that the world loses its hold, holiness and purity are manifested and society is *changed.*

Revival preaching is marked by a return to the basic tenets of the Gospel — a return to the preaching of the *cross* of Christ, a return to preaching about the *blood of the Lamb!* We've racked up a lot of numbers, but how many of those at the altar have truly been *convicted* of sin. How many of us *really* know, in the *depths* of our being, how *lost* we were and how *great* the love of God is toward us?

Conviction Warns of Danger

Conviction of the Holy Ghost is to our spirit what *pain* is to our body. Pain is not an enemy in itself. It is only an indication that the enemy exists. Without pain a person could stroll barefoot down a sandy beach, step on a broken glass, cut a big gash in his foot and go merrily on his way and bleed to death.

Conviction is like pain — it warns us when there is danger in our path, or when we have stepped into something harmful. Conviction reminds us of where we *came from* so we can fully appreciate where we *are.* We were *lost*, but now we are *found*. We were strangers and aliens from the covenants of promise, having no hope, without God in the world. But now, *in Christ Jesus* we who once were far off are brought near to God. (Eph. 2:12, 13.)

It is wonderful to know our position in Christ. It is wonderful to have righteousness consciousness. But we must never forget where we came *from*. It is not until we have really realized how *lost* we were that we can realize and appreciate the depth of the love of God in Christ. It is by understanding the depravity of sin and our own hopeless state that we can fully appreciate the goodness of God that led us to repentance and eternal life.

The Fear of the Lord

O fear the Lord, ye his saints: for there is no want to them that fear him.

Psalm 34:9

Much of the Church has lost the fear of the Lord. Some have forgotten what it means to reverence a holy God. Much of the Church has an ungodly arrogance born of a gospel of humanism.

God is different from us. He is *"other"* than we are. Through Him we are made pure — He *is* purity. Through Him we are made holy — He *is* holy. Through Him we have joy — He *is* joy. Through Him we are healed — He *is* healing. God is the very essence and substance of the things we come to His throne for, yet we often approach Him with a careless arrogance.

We Have Traded Boldness for Arrogance

Some have traded holy boldness for fleshly arrogance and godly piety for human pride. They talk about their position in Christ, then talk about their neighbor or pastor. They gossip, ridicule, cheat their brothers, indulge in sexual sin and compromise with the world, then come to Church and raise their sin-stained hands to a holy God.

The voice of God is calling us to make ourselves clean — to wash our hands and our garments in the blood of the Lamb. He is calling us to be like Paul who counted all things as loss — *worthless* — compared to the prize of *knowing Christ Jesus*.

The Church must look beyond the agenda of man and the programs of the world. The Church must go beyond her so-called giftings. It is time we stop leaning on the crutch of our own ability and humble ourselves under the mighty hand of an Almighty God.

This is what revival is all about. Revival is when men rend their hearts in the presence of God. Revival is when men take off their masks, realize their lost and lowly estate and exalt a holy and righteous God.

Someone has suggested that if the Holy Spirit were to withdraw from the earth, ninety percent of all so-called Christian activity would go on unchanged. We say we sing to God, but we sing for ourselves. We say we preach to save souls, but most preaching is to satisfy ourselves and build our own kingdoms.

God Is Calling for Radical Change

Much of the Church has her head in the lap of Delilah, thinking, like Samson, that she can get up one more time and shake off her enemies. But God is calling us to repentance and separation from the world lest we awaken one day and find the anointing gone, the power gone, and, like Samson, not even know the Spirit of God is gone.

There must be a radical change in the Church today — as radical as when we were born again. We must cry out from our hearts, ''O God, *change* us. *Change us lest we perish!*'' We should be crying out for the presence of God to so permeate our lives that when we take one step in a contrary direction we will immediately sense the righteous conviction of God.

The Church must get out of the deception of thinking all is well and God's presence is among us. We must radically change our thinking, and realize that we cannot contaminate our bodies, the temple of God, with the filth of the world and expect to come into the presence of a holy God. If His presence *was* manifested the way we pray for it, it would consume us because of our unrepentant sin and arrogance.

Revival is coming, but before it can come, there must be a return to holiness and sanctification. The mercy of God waits for the Church to judge herself and return to preaching and *living* holiness, that when He comes as a consuming fire, He will find only gold, silver and precious stones to refine and purify, not wood, hay and stubble to consume.

GOD IS BUILDING A HABITATION

8

God Is Building a Habitation

> Ye also, as lively stones, are built up a spiritual
> house, an holy priesthood, to offer up spiritual
> sacrifices, acceptable to God by Jesus Christ.
>
> 1 Peter 2:5

God is doing a work in the midst of His people. He
is building a holy habitation in which He will dwell and we,
the Church, are those lively stones built up into the spiritual
house where God's Spirit abides.

The cry of my heart is for those who are sleeping in
the Church to awaken from their lethargy and selfishness
and realize that a holy God has chosen *us* for His holy
habitation. I pray with Paul (Eph. 1:17,18) for the whole
Body of Christ:

> That the God of our Lord Jesus Christ, the Father
> of glory, may give unto you the spirit of wisdom and
> revelation in the knowledge of him:
>
> The eyes of your understanding being
> enlightened; that ye may know what is the hope of his
> calling, and what the riches of the glory of his
> inheritance in the saints.

God is doing a work in His people. He has prepared
this time, this place and this people, His Church, to receive
a word from Him which will send revival across this nation.
The Church must hear with spirit ears and see with spirit
eyes what the Lord is doing in this hour, and not let *anything*
— demons, people, cares of this world or anything else —
distract her from what God is saying in this hour. It is a
season of turning — a season of change.

71

With Oswald Chambers let our hearts cry out, "If this is all there is to Christianity, then the whole thing must be a fraud. If I can't walk with God in a greater capacity than I'm walking with Him today — if I can't sense God to a greater degree than I am sensing Him today — if I cannot understand His Word greater and to a higher dimension and deeper depth than I understand it today, then the whole thing is a fraud. The Bible is just an ordinary book, and Jesus was just a prophet and a good man that came to teach us how to be nice."

But Jesus is more than a good man. Jesus is more than a prophet. Jesus is the son of the holy, living God. We must no longer take His Word as a light thing. We must not take the assembling of ourselves together as a light thing. We are the holy sanctuary of God and He is assembling us into a holy habitation where His Spirit dwells.

Old Testament Types and Shadows

We see types and shadows throughout the Word of God that point to the habitation God is building. In 2 Kings 4:8-11 we read of the Shunammite woman who built a special chamber in her home for the prophet Elisha when he passed through.

She was building a room for the prophet, who represented God at that time. She wanted a place for God to dwell. That is what God is doing in the Church today. He is building a place where He can dwell — not just a place to stop by for a visit now and then, but a place He will live in *permanently*.

We will never be satisfied with a God Who drops by occasionally and manifests His glory. There should be a hunger in the people of God that we be fitted, framed and cleaned up for a holy habitation for the Master. The Church, individually and collectively, should be crying out to God for every impurity, everything that offends Him to be removed — that He would come, not just for an occasional visit, but for a permanent habitation.

Jesus Stands and Knocks
at the Door of the Church

The Bible declares that we have this treasure, this Holy Ghost, living on the inside of us. But like the Church at Laodicea, much of today's Church has shut itself off and closed the door to the habitation of God.

Traditionally, preachers have used Revelation 3:20 as an altar call to sinners:

> **Behold, I stand at the door, and knock: if any man hear my voice, and open the door, I will come in to him, and will sup with him, and he with me.**

We have painted a picture of Jesus standing at the door of the unregenerate, unrepentant heart of a vile sinner, inviting him to salvation. But this was not written to a vile sinner who did not know or acknowledge Jesus. This was written to the *Church.* Jesus is knocking on the door of His own house, crying "Let Me in!" He is not knocking on a door of wood, stone, brick and mortar. He is knocking on the door of His *living* house, built out of *living stones.*

God Is a God of Diversity

Psalm 19:1 says: **The heavens declare the glory of God; and the firmament sheweth his handiwork.**

We can look at nature and see the changing colors of the seasons, the infinite variety of plants and animals and the horizon ablaze with the glory of a celestial God, and we begin to understand the handiwork of God in building His Church.

If you give man a seed, he will plant an orchard, lined up neatly in rows, all looking the same and all bearing the same fruit. But God takes seeds and plants forests of infinite variety.

The spiritual house that God is building — the Church — is made up of stones of infinite variety. We are not all out of the same mold. We don't all look and talk and act alike. We cannot presume to tell God what stones to use or how to build His house. *He* is the Master Builder.

We must break out of our traditional religious thinking and divisive doctrines and let God build *His* house the way *He* wants it. God wants to show forth His glory and power in an unprecedented manner. He wants to display, *through the Church*, signs and wonders that will stagger modern man. But in order to do that, He first must build a house that will *contain* His glory.

God Wants To Live In His People

God told Moses to build the tabernacle according to certain specifications, and He would come and display His glory there. Moses, Aaron and the priests would come and meet in the door of the tent and the power of God would be so awesome that the priest could not stand to minister. The cloud of the glory of God dwelt in that tent.

We have had bursts of that glory in our day. We have had manifestations of revival here and there. And we have seen men preach in the absolute cloud of His glory and then go out and practice immorality or some other sin. How can this happen? Because we have not practiced an *awareness* of His presence to the point that His glory dwells among us.

Psalm 16:8 says:

I have set the Lord always before me: because he is at my right hand, I shall not be moved.

This is what it means to get our eyes off the world and off our problems. When we set the Lord always before us — when we know we are a stone in His hand being fashioned into His dwelling place — then it is harder to sin. When we are continually beholding the presence of God, sin must go and stay away! It is hard to lie, cheat, steal or commit adultery when we are continually beholding the face of God and living in His presence.

Presence Beheld Becomes Presence Revealed

Presence beheld becomes presence revealed! As we look into His glory, we are changed into His likeness. (2 Cor. 3:18.) Yes, we will see cripples by the thousands leap out of their wheelchairs. We will see altar calls with tens of thousands of people running into the presence of God. *But we will never see the move of God visibly in power until we have first allowed him to move invisibly in holiness.*

There are preachers trying desperately to get a miracle in their ministry. But we don't need a miracle. We just need to behold Him, like a little child. We need to humbly prepare our hearts for a habitation He can dwell in, and we will have all the miracles and power we can handle.

Jesus is knocking on the door of our hearts, wanting in. We may be saved, but is Jesus the *Lord* of our lives? Are we moved and swayed by the opinions of others, or is our gaze fastened on the One who shed His blood on Calvary?

God Wants Intimacy

The one thing most needed in the Church today — the thing many Christians never achieve — is *intimacy* with God. We need to speak honestly with God. We need God intimately involved in our marriages, businesses, families, friendships and ministries.

Many people do not know how to open their innermost hearts to God on a personal, private level. We often do not trust God enough to do this because we simply have not spent enough *time* with Him to get to know Him. An intimate relationship cannot be built in a group. We can't get it at the Sunday morning service. An intimate relationship of total trust will only come in our personal, private times of prayer, meditation in the Word and listening to Him speak to our spirit man.

People seek intimacy everywhere but with God, and it will never be fulfilled. There is a vacuum on the inside of many Christians that only communion with a holy God can fill. It can't be filled by a spouse, a friend, a lover, drugs or money. It can't be filled by religion, tapes or meetings, either. The *only* thing that will fill this vacuum is climbing the heights of the mountain of God and there communing with Him as we behold His presence.

Intimacy Demands Prayer

To have intimacy with God, we must have regular times alone with Him. We must have time where we get away from our jobs, our families, our ministries and the cares of the world and talk to God openly and honestly — and *allow Him to talk honestly to us.* We have to be willing for Him to build His house the way He wants to.

We want God to build His house, but we often want to rearrange it every day. He builds a wall and we tear it down. He tears down a wall and we build it back up. It is time for us to humbly lay ourselves on the potter's wheel and let Him mold and make what He wants. It is time to let God build His holy habitation in us. When He does the building to His specifications, He will come and dwell, and His glory will be revealed.

Where is the Church who will go before God and say, ''God, take out of me what You do not want and put in what You do want. You know more about this than we do. All we want is to become a habitation for You to live in. We want to behold Your glory, because when we *behold* your glory, we will *manifest* Your glory.''

God Is Preparing a Bride

God is preparing a bride for His Son. No bride would come to her wedding with the gown stained and wrinkled.

Brides come to weddings fresh and clean, with a perfect gown, and every detail perfectly worked out.

We are the bride of Christ, and we are in the final preparation stages for the wedding supper. It is the time and season to get the wrinkles out, to clean the spots in the blood of the Lamb and to wash ourselves in the water of the Word.

Are we hearers of the Word and not doers? Do we conduct ourselves in a manner worthy of the Lord, thinking on the things that are pure, lovely, honest and of good report? Have we been cleansed by the blood of the Lamb and washed in the water of the Word?

God is preparing a habitation for His glory — His abiding presence — to dwell in. His grace has chosen us, the Church, to be the tabernacle for His Spirit, the bride for His Son, the eternal city which will radiate His glory to the nations.

God says in Malachi 3:1:

Behold, I will send my messenger, and he shall prepare the way before me: and the Lord, whom ye seek, shall suddenly come to his temple, even the messenger of the covenant, whom ye delight in: behold, he shall come, saith the Lord of hosts.

We are the temple, and the Spirit of the Lord is calling to us to get the temple ready, because He is coming. He wants His Church to allow Him to take the searchlight of His Word and Spirit and shine inside the darkened recesses of our hearts to examine methods and motives, and remove anything that is contrary to His will and purpose.

The call to the Church in this hour is to *behold* Him, to *know* Him and to *allow* Him to change us into His glory and likeness. Jesus calls us to forsake the methods and manners of the world and return to our first love. Our challenge is to separate ourselves from the world and unto

God, and walk in holiness and reverence before Him, that He might manifest Himself *in* us and *through* us to a lost and dying world.

Rod Parsley began his ministry as an energetic 21-year-old in the backyard of his parent's Ohio home. The fresh, "old-time gospel" approach of Parsley's delivery immediately attracted a hungry, God-seeking audience. From the 17 people who attended that first 1977 backyard meeting, the crowds grew rapidly.

Today, as the pastor of Columbus, Ohio's 5,200-seat World Harvest Church, Parsley oversees World Harvest's K-12 Christian Academy; a Spirit-led Bible Institute; and numerous church sponsored outreaches including "Lifeline," a pro-life organization, "Lightline," an anti-pornography league, and "Breakthrough," World Harvest Church's national television broadcast reaching over 100 million people.

Pastor Rod Parsley also serves as Dr. Lester Sumrall's personal assistant in directing the End-Time "Feed The Hungry" program.

To contact Rod Parsley, write:

World Harvest Church • P. O. Box 32932
Columbus, OH 43232 • U. S. A.

Additional copies of this book are available
from your local bookstore or from:

Harrison House
P. O. Box 35035 • Tulsa, OK 74153

For additional copies of
this book in Canada contact:

Word Alive • P.O. Box 284
Niverville, Manitoba • CANADA R0A 1EO

For international sales in Europe, contact:

Harrison House Europe • Belruptstrasse 42 A
A - 6900 Bregenz • AUSTRIA

The Harrison House Vision

Proclaiming the truth and power
Of the Gospel of Jesus Christ
With excellence;

Challenging Christians to
Live victoriously,
Grow spiritually,
Know God intimately.